James Payn

Westminster Cook-Book

Every recipe tried and proved. 183 Receipes

James Payn

Westminster Cook-Book
Every recipe tried and proved. 183 Receipes

ISBN/EAN: 9783744788984

Printed in Europe, USA, Canada, Australia, Japan

Cover: Foto ©Lupo / pixelio.de

More available books at **www.hansebooks.com**

WESTMINSTER

COOK-BOOK.

EVERY RECIPE TRIED AND PROVED.

We may live without poetry, music, and art
We may live without conscience, and live without heart.
We may live without friends, we may live without books.
But what civilized man can live without cooks?

He may live without books—what is knowledge but grieving?
He may live without hope—what is hope but deceiving?
He may live without love—what is passion but pining?
But where is the man that can live without dining?

ONE HUNDRED AND EIGHTY-THREE RECIPES.

PHILADELPHIA:
HOLLOWBUSH AND CAREY,
423 MARKET STREET.
1876.

SOUPS.

Soups.

We have deemed it unnecessary to give recipes for the common every-day soups. Beef and veal form the stock, with such vegetables and herbs as suit the tastes of the household. For *white* soups veal is best; for *brown*, use beef and the bones and trimmings of other meats and poultry. Always use *cold* water, and after it begins to boil, place it in a position where it will *simmer* only, but be sure to *keep it simmering* for four or five hours, with the pot closely covered. In winter, sufficient stock may be made to last several days, and this quantity should boil all day. A portion can be used with sliced vegetables as vegetable soup, one day; with vermicelli, another day; and again, with tomatoes and the addition of a little catsup as tomato soup. To color soups, use for thickening flour that has been previously browned in the oven.

Clam Soup.

To a gallon of cut-up clams and their liquor, well boiled and strained, put a cup and a half of cream, two tablespoonsful of flour creamed with a quarter of a pound of butter, and well seasoned with salt, pepper, and mace.

Crab Soup.

Three dozen crabs boiled and picked, divide them equally, boil again one half in a full gallon of water, with salt and mace, for about an hour. Then take off and strain, put the soup on again with a teacup of cream, quarter of a pound of butter, two and a half tablespoonsful of flour creamed with the butter and scalded with a little of the hot soup, a tablespoonful of mixed mustard, black and red pepper. Have in your tureen the remaining dozen and a half crabs cleanly picked, and pour the hot soup upon them, and serve without delay, for it is delicious.

Oyster Soup.

One and a half cups of cream to a gallon of oysters and liquor, two tablespoonsful of flour, creamed with a quarter of a pound of butter and well seasoned with pepper, salt, and mace.

MEATS.

Asparagus.

Take two bunches of freshly gathered asparagus, cut in small pieces, and boil until tender in water enough to cover it, having first put into this water one dessertspoonful of sugar. Then add one pint of milk, butter, pepper, and salt to taste, and let it *just* come up to a boil.

Be sure and *not boil it.* Serve in deep plates.

Baked Ham.

Boil until quite done, then remove the skin. Rub together one teaspoon cayenne pepper, two of ground cloves, two of grated nutmeg, two tablespoons of brown sugar. Make incisions with a knife all over the top the depth of the fat, into which force the mixture. The balance must be rubbed over the top, then cover the surface thickly with bread crumbs. Bake slowly about one-half hour, basting frequently with the essence to keep it from burning.

Corn Oysters.

Grate down twelve ears of corn, beat two eggs very light, stir well together with pepper and salt, add two tablespoons of powdered cracker, fry in lard.

1*

Croquettes.

Having chopped fine your meat, take some grated bread crumbs, and season with salt, pepper, mace, nutmeg, and grated lemon rind. Moisten the whole with cream, and make into small cones. Have ready some beaten eggs, mix with grated bread, dip into it each croquette and fry slowly in butter.

Deviled Crabs.

One dozen crabs, a small loaf of baker's bread, three teaspoonsful of mixed mustard, two of black pepper, half a teaspoonful of cayenne, and one of salt, teacup of vinegar, and five ounces of butter. Bake in shells.

Drawn Butter.

Mix two or three teaspoonsful of flour with a little cold water, stir until clear of lumps, thin it, and pour on a half pint of boiling water, stirring constantly. Boil it two or three minutes; then cut up four ounces of butter in it, and melt and stir; add hard-boiled eggs sliced or minced as desired.

Mock Oysters.

A pint of boiled hominy, two eggs, a teacup of flour, a tablespoonful of butter (melted), pepper and salt to taste; mix all well together, make in little cakes and fry a light brown.

Mock Terrapin.

Season and fry brown a calf's liver, then hash it fine, dust thickly with flour. two tablespoonsful of mixed mustard, a little cayenne pepper, three hard-boiled eggs chopped fine, a piece of butter the size of an egg, and a teacup of water. Let it simmer a few minutes, then serve hot.

Omelet.

Three teaspoonsful of fresh milk to each egg, a little salt, beat the eggs light, add the milk, and cook, stirring all the time.

Slaw Dressing.

The yolks of two eggs well beaten, two teaspoonsful of sugar, one of mustard, one of salt, one of black pepper, beat all together; add one teacup of cream or milk, and half a cup of vinegar. Set on the fire and stir until it becomes as thick as boiled custard. Let it come to a boil.

Spiced Beef.

Four pounds of tender beef minced fine, one pound suet chopped fine, mix them together; one spoonful of cloves, half the quantity of pepper, salt to your taste, a teacup of water. Mix all together, then pack in a tin pan the size to suit the quantity. Put in the oven and bake an hour and a half. This is a delightful relish for tea, cut thin.

Sausage Meat.

To twenty-nine pounds of chopped meat, add eleven ounces of salt, nine heaped tablespoonsful of freshly rubbed sage, five tablespoonsful of ground black pepper. If cayenne pepper is liked, put to this a half teaspoonful of ground cayenne.

Sauce for Cold Meats.

Boil two eggs three minutes, mix a small teaspoonful of mixed mustard, a little pepper and salt—six spoonsful of drawn butter or oil, six of vinegar, and one of catsup.

Turkey or Chicken Patties.

Mince fine your cold fowl, together with some cold boiled ham or tongue; add the yolks of hard-boiled eggs grated, a little cayenne pepper, some powdered mace, and nutmeg. Mix and moisten with cream or butter. Have ready some puff paste in pattypans, and fill with the mixture. Add oysters, and warm with hot shovel.

Tomato Beef.

Take five pounds of beef off the end of the surloin, place it in a pot with sufficient water to keep it from burning, and *no more*. It should be turned often, let it brown, cook one hour, then add twelve tomatoes, half an onion chopped fine, pepper and salt. After adding the tomatoes, stew one hour longer. Serve the beef with the tomatoes around it.

Turkey Sauce.

Mix two or three teaspoonsful of flour with a little cold milk, stir it until clear of lumps, thin it and pour on a half-pint of boiling milk, stirring constantly. Boil it two or three minutes. Then cut up four ounces of butter in it, melt, and stir and add one pint of oysters and celery chopped.

Veal Patties.

Three pounds of veal, one pound and a half of fresh pork, quarter of a pound of butter, and four eggs. Grind the meat fine, add the other ingredients. Season to taste with mustard, pepper, and salt. Roll into shape. Set them in the oven and brown over. To be eaten cold.

BREADS.

Bridgeton Rolls.

One quart of new milk, one cup and a half of lard and butter mixed, two eggs, two table-spoonsful of sugar, one and a half cups of yeast, and a little salt; make up soft, let them rise, and make them out two hours before you bake them.

Corn Muffins.

One quart of milk, one and a half pints flour (even measure), one-half that quantity of meal, sift both together, five eggs beaten very light (yolks and whites separately), and added to the batter, a little salt; butter small tin muffin *pans* (not rings), bake in a quick oven from twenty to twenty-five minutes.

Flannel Cakes.

Take three eggs, half-pint of milk, melt there-in a tablespoonful of lard, then add half-pint cold water, and one teacup of yeast, mix all together, and make the batter as thick as for buckwheat cakes.

Laplanders.

Beat two eggs very light, then add one pint milk, one pint flour, one teaspoon salt, beat well together, and bake in small tins. This quantity makes one dozen. Have the tins *hot.*

Light Bread.

For two loaves of bread, thicken one quart of lukewarm water with flour until it will just pour easily, add one tablespoonful of salt, half teacup yeast; this should be done about 7 P. M. About 10 P. M. work in flour until it is nearly as stiff as pie crust, and let it rise again in a mass; it will rise high and crack open. When it is sufficiently light, mould it into loaves, and let it stand about an hour, when it will be ready to bake, which you can tell by its cracking open. The flour should always be sifted, and the dough well kneaded.

Light Biscuit.

Two pounds of flour, quarter of a pound of lard, one pint of milk, and a cup of yeast, and a little salt. To be made in the evening if intended for breakfast, or in the morning for tea.

Maryland Biscuit.

Take two quarts of flour, one-quarter pound lard, and a little salt. Mix with as little water

as possible, and then knead it until soft.   Break
up into pieces, and roll into shape, prick with a
fork, and bake them in a quick oven.   To be
good, they must be worked a great deal.

Muffin Bread.

Make up over night just as you would light
bread only softer, adding two eggs, a mixed
spoonful of butter and lard, one teaspoon of
sugar at the time you make it up.   Mould out
only in one loaf as you would rolls, and let it
rise again before baking.   Bake in a pie plate
(it is stiff enough not to run over).   Split in
half, butter, lay lightly together again, and send
to the table hot.   Serve in quarters.

Muffins.

Take three eggs, half pint of milk and water
in equal quantities, melt therein a tablespoonful of lard, then add half pint cold water, one
teacup of yeast, mix all together and stir in
flour to make it a thick fritter batter.

Quick Light Cake for Breakfast.

Mix dry and well rubbed together two teaspoonsful of cream of tartar, with one quart of
flour, then dissolve three-quarters of a teaspoonful of super-carbonate of soda in a suffi-

cient quantity of sweet milk (about a pint),
mix the whole together, and bake immediately.
Split and butter. Serve while hot.

Sally Lunn.

One pint of milk, three eggs, one quart of
flour, half a teacup of yeast. Put this to rise,
and when light beat in one cup of melted butter.
Then put it into your pan or pans, and let it
rise again, and bake when light.

Sally Lunn (with yeast).

Warm one quart of milk with quarter pound
of butter, two heaping tablespoons of sugar,
half a nutmeg. Beat up three eggs and put
in, with a little salt, and flour enough to make
it stiffer than pound cake. Beat it well. Add
a teacup of yeast, and let it rise. Butter a
fluted cake mould and pour it in Bake in a
quick oven one hour.

If you wish tea at 7 o'clock, set it to rise at
11 A.M.

Sally Lunn (without yeast).

One quart of flour, a piece of butter the size
of an egg, three tablespoons of sugar, two eggs,
two teacups milk, two teaspoons of cream of
tartar, one teaspoon of saleratus, a little salt.

2

To mix it scatter the cream of tartar, the salt, and the sugar into the flour. Add the eggs without having beaten them, the butter melted, and one cup of the milk. Dissolve the saleratus in the remaining cup, and then stir all together steadily a few minutes. This makes two loaves. Add spice and twice the measure of sugar, and you have a good plain cake for the cake basket.

Supper Fritters.

One and a half cups of sugar beaten with three eggs, one cup of sour cream, and one and a half cups of buttermilk, in which stir a teaspoonful of soda. Add flour enough to make a thin muflin-batter, and fry.

Tea Cake.

One pint of milk, two eggs, half cup of butter, half cup of yeast. Make this into a rising, and when light knead in sufficient flour to make as stiff as roll dough. Make this into three flat cakes, and let it rise again.

Wafers or Wine Crackers.

Three pints of flour, one heaping tablespoonful of lard, one tablespoonful of salt. Rub the flour, lard, and salt well together. Make up quite stiff. Knead them till soft. Break into small pieces and roll them out as thin as wafers. Prick with a fork before placing in the oven.

Wheat Muffins.

Early in the morning take off a piece of light dough, say what has been made from one quart of flour. Thin this to the consistency of batter by the addition of sweet milk. After beating it till smooth, let it rise all together for one hour; then on a delicately greased griddle drop the batter from a spoon, and, as soon as lightly browned on one side, turn on the other. Serve up hot, and tear open instead of cutting with a knife.

Yeast.

One cup of hops, two quarts of water boiled down to one quart, five potatoes boiled and mashed, one cup of flour. Mix the potatoes and flour together, strain the hop-water over them. Put on the stove and let it boil a few minutes, then set it aside to cool. When cool add one cup of brown sugar and one cup of yeast. It will keep sweet several weeks.

CAKES.

A Cheap Cake.

Four eggs, three cups of flour, two cups of sugar, one cup of milk, half cup of butter, two and a half teaspoonsful of yeast powder. Flavor with almonds, and bake in a quick oven.

Albany Cakes.

One and a half pounds of flour, one pound of sugar, half pound of butter, one quarter of an ounce of cinnamon, one tablespoonful of lard, one teacup of cream, one teaspoonful of saleratus, and one wineglass of rose-water.

Butter Cake.

To one pint of warm milk add half a pound of butter, the same of sugar, and four eggs well beaten, the rind of one lemon, a nutmeg, a teaspoonful of salt, one cup of yeast, and flour enough to make a stiff batter. If put to rise in the evening, it will be ready to bake in the morning. Put it in your baking pans half inch thick, and set it to rise a second time; when light, put small pieces of butter over the top, and sift cinnamon and sugar, then it is ready for the oven.

Caromel.

Three pounds sugar, one and a half cakes chocolate, half a pound butter, two cups milk, one small bottle extract of vanilla. Boil until it thickens, stirring constantly. Pour on buttered plates and bar off.

Centennial Cake.

One pound of sugar, half pound of butter, cream the butter and sugar together, six eggs. Break in an egg, and add a handful of flour, and so on until you get the eggs in; then add a glass of ice-water and more flour until it is as stiff as pound cake; flavor to taste, and put into the flour a tablespoonful of yeast powder.

Children's Cakes.

One and a half pounds of flour, three-quarters of a pound of sugar, six ounces of butter, one nutmeg and a half, one and a half small tea-cupsful of milk, two teaspoonsful of yeast powder, one and a half tablespoonsful of brandy, and the same of rose-water.

Chocolate Cake.

Two cups sugar, two-thirds cup of butter, two cups flour, yolks and whites of six eggs

2*

beaten separately, one teaspoon cream of tartar, half teaspoon soda dissolved in half cup sweet milk. Bake in layers. Half pound Baker's chocolate grated fine in half pint milk, flavor and sweeten to taste. Boil this for a few minutes until it thickens. While cooling add one egg well beaten. Spread the chocolate upon the cake as soon as taken from the oven (as you would jelly cake).

Chocolate Cake.

One pound of sugar, one pound of flour, half a pound of butter, six eggs, one cup of milk, three teaspoonsful of yeast powder.

Icing—three-quarters of a pound of chocolate, grated and mixed with four tablespoonsful of milk, put in the oven to melt, and when melted mix with icing the same as white mountain cake. This quantity makes two large cakes.

Coffee Cake.

One pint of sponge, half a pint of milk, one-quarter pound of butter, one-quarter pound of lard, add the milk, stir in the sponge, one-half pound of brown sugar, two eggs. Scald the raisins or currants, wipe them dry, flavor to your taste with spice; thicken until the spoon stands in the batter. Make up the sponge the night before, add the ingredients the next morning, and it will be fit to bake for tea.

Cream Cake.

One tablespoonful of butter, one cup of sugar, two-thirds of a cup of sweet milk, one egg, two teaspoonsful of cream tartar, one of soda, one and two-third cups of flour, flavor with vanilla or lemon, and bake in layers as for jelly cake.

Cup Cake.

Two cups of white sugar stirred into one cup of butter until quite light, three cups of sifted flour, four eggs beaten light (whites and yolks separately); beat the yolks into the sugar and butter, stir the flour in gently, one cup of milk, one teaspoonful of soda, one of cream of tartar, lastly the whites; beat all well, bake in a moderate oven in small tins, sift sugar over them.

Cup Cake.

Three cups of sugar, one of butter, four of flour, one of cream, three eggs, one teaspoonful of pearlash; let these ingredients be well beaten together, and add spice to your taste.

Cup Cake.

One cup of cream, two cups of butter, three cups of sugar, and four cups of flour, five eggs, and spice to your taste ; bake thin.

Caromel.

Three pounds of sugar, one cake of chocolate, half pint of cream, quarter of a pound of butter. Season with vanilla. Boil slowly about thirty minutes, as it burns easily.

Delicate Cake.

One and a half cups sugar, half cup butter, two cups flour, four eggs, half cup milk, two teaspoons baking powder in the flour.

Doughnuts.

Four pounds and a half of flour, two and a half pounds of sugar, six eggs beaten light, three half pints of milk (warmed), one pound of lard, and two tablespoonsful of good yeast. Mix all into a soft dough, let them stand two hours before they are rolled, then melt two pounds of lard in a kettle, and throw in a few at a time. They quickly bake if the lard is scalding hot.

English Cake.

Take five eggs, then the weight of five eggs in sugar, the weight of four in flour, the weight of three in butter, one nutmeg, and a glass of wine.

Everton Taffy.

One pound of sugar, two tablespoonsful of vinegar; soak twelve hours, then add a small lump of butter and boil; flavor with vanilla.

Federal Cakes.

One pound of flour, six ounces of butter, the same of sugar, well rubbed together with half a teaspoonful of spice, one egg well beaten, one-quarter glass of rose-water, and six drops of essence of lemon. Bake in small cakes.

French Custard Cake.

Four eggs, one and a half pints of milk, lump of butter the size of a walnut, three table-spoons corn-starch, one lemon, sugar, and flavoring to taste.

Fruit Cake.

One pound of butter, one pound of sugar, one pound of flour, two and a half pounds of raisins, two and a half pounds of currants, one pound of citron, twelve eggs, four nutmegs, one tablespoon of cinnamon, one wineglass of rose-water, one of brandy, two of wine.

Gen. Lee Cake.

Make by gold cake recipe, putting into the batter the grated rind of two oranges. Bake in white cake tins, and put, when cold, icing between and over it.

Icing for above.—Take the juice of two oranges and one lemon, into which put as much pulverized sugar as will make very stiff. This is excellent for any other cake.

Ginger Bread.

Two pounds of flour, one pound and a quarter of sugar, one pound of butter, and a spoonful of lard, nine eggs, nearly a cup of ginger, and either a half-cup of cinnamon or two nutmegs, and a desertspoonful of mace, a small teaspoonful of soda in milk or cream, a pint of molasses.

Ginger Cup-Cake.

One cup butter, one cup molasses, one cup sugar, three eggs, three cups flour, one teaspoon saleratus, one tablespoon ginger; bake in pans. A pound of stoned and chopped raisins is an improvement.

Ginger Cakes.

One pint of molasses, one cup of sugar, three-quarters of a pound of lard and butter mixed, one tablespoonful of ginger, one teaspoonful of cinnamon, and one of salt, flour enough to make it stiff.

General Directions for Lightening

In measuring yeast powder for any recipe in this book, be sure to *heap* the teaspoon, or the quantity will be insufficient to produce the desired lightness. The proper manner to lighten eggs is to whisk the whites first to a *stiff* froth, and then gradually whip the yolks into it.

Ginger Snaps.

One cup of molasses, one cup of sugar, one cup of milk, one cup of butter, one and a half tablespoonsful of ginger, quarter of a teaspoonful of soda, and a half teaspoonful of cream tartar, one teaspoonful of salt, and flour to make stiff enough to roll out.

Gold Cake.

Take the yelks of the fourteen eggs left from white cake, put them in a pint measure, and fill to the top with new milk. Beat well, and when

light, add alternately with one pound of sifted
flour, to one pound of sugar and three-quarters
of a pound of butter (creamed). Flavor with
one wineglass of brandy, one of wine, and whatever spice or extract you desire for flavoring.
Put into the flour three teaspoonsful of yeast
powder. Bake one hour and a half if made in
a large cake.

Good Rusks and Doughnuts.

Into a pint of milk, put three cups of sugar
and a bit of butter the size of an egg. Set it on
the stove until the butter is entirely melted.
When cool, add half pint of yeast and four well-
beaten eggs. Cinnamon or nutmeg to taste,
and as much flour as will make it as thick
as muffin dough. Set to rise all night. In the
morning work in flour enough to make like soft
bread dough, and make half into rusks which
may sit two or three hours longer to rise.
When nicely baked, rub over with butter, on
which sprinkle cinnamon and sugar quite thick.
The remaining half of dough may be rolled out
(after the rusks are baked), and cut into shapes,
and fried in boiling lard. Sprinkle while hot
with pulverized sugar, and cinnamon if liked.

Indian Meal Cakes.

One pound of meal, one pound of Havana sugar, half pound of butter, beat butter and sugar to a cream, take out one handful of meal and add one of wheat flour, four eggs. Rosewater, and spice to your taste. Drop them on tin sheets or bake them in very small tins.

Jelly Cake.

One cup of butter, two cups of sugar, three cups of flour, whites of seven eggs, and one cup of milk.

Jelly Cake.

Ten eggs, three-quarters pound sifted flour, one pound white sugar, juice and rind of one lemon. Separate the eggs, beat the yolks very light, then add the sugar, then the whites, and finally stir in the flour gently. Bake in eight layers.

Jumbles.

One cup butter, two cups sugar, one teacup milk, five eggs, one teaspoon soda dissolved in boiling water, one teaspoon of nutmeg, sufficient flour to make a soft dough. Roll out, cut into shapes, and sift sugar over them before they go into the oven.

3

Jumbles.

One pound of flour, three-quarters of a pound of butter, the same of sugar, two eggs beaten very light, a little nutmeg and cinnamon, one tablespoonful of rose-water.

Lee Cake.

Bake sponge cakes in jelly pans. Grate the rind of a lemon and squeeze the juice, grate a large orange and add to the lemon, then stir in one pound of granulated sugar till it becomes thick. Spread this between the layers of cake while hot.

Light Wigs.

Two pounds of flour, four eggs, one-quarter of a pound of butter, one-half pound of sugar, one pint of milk, a coffee-cup of yeast, and a little nutmeg.

Little Pine Cakes.

One pound of flour, half pound of sugar, and the same of butter; beat to a cream. Mix well together, and bake in small tins.

London Coffee Cake.

Four eggs, half pound of butter, half pound of sugar, half pint of rich milk, one pound of flour, into which rub two teaspoonsful o" yeast-powder. Bake like Sally Lunn. Just before you take it from the oven sprinkle pulverized sugar over the top, and cinnamon if you like.

Love Cakes.

Mix with twelve egg yolks a glass of rose-water, four ounces of bitter almonds finely pow-dered, and sugar enough to make a batter stiff enough to bake in boxes.

Maccaroons.

One pint ground-nuts or almonds well beaten, one pint of sugar, whites of five eggs whipped-up, flour enough to stick together. Bake in little pans or on white paper in a moderate oven.

Marbled Cake.

One cup of butter, two cups of powdered sugar, three cups of flour, four eggs, one cup of sweet milk, one-half a teaspoonful of soda, one of cream of tartar, sifted with the flour. When the cake is mixed, take out about one teacup of batter, and stir into this a large spoonful of grated chocolate, wet with a scant tablespoon-ful of milk. Fill the mould about one inch deep with the yellow batter, then drop on this in two or three places a spoonful of the dark mixture;

give the brown spots a light stir with the top
of the spoon, spreading it in broken circles
upon the lighter surface. Proceed in this order
until it is used up. When cut the cake will be
handsomely variegated. The reserved cupful
of batter may be colored with enough prepared
cochineal to give it a fine pink tint, and mix as
you do the brown.

Marvels.

Beat two eggs very light, add one pint of
flour, a little salt, and two dessertspoonsful of
water. Fry them in hot lard, and sprinkle
sugar over them when done.

Montrose Cakes.

One cup of sugar, two eggs, one cup of sweet
milk, one tablespoonful of butter, one teaspoonful of yeast-powder, and four cups of flour.

Orange Cake.

Mix well together one pound of sugar and
three-quarters of a pound of butter; when light
add eight eggs; mix well, and flavor with extract of orange; then add three-quarters of a
pound of sifted flour, and stir until the dough
becomes smooth; put in one or more pans, and
bake.

Parkton Rusk.

Two cups of sugar, four ounces of butter, four eggs, one nutmeg; cream the sugar and butter together, then put in the nutmegs, and add the eggs, and when well mixed stir in one cup of yeast and one cup of warm water, and thicken with a pound and a quarter of flour, and set it to rise. This should be done about noon, and at night work into the rising a pound and a quarter more of flour, and put it again to lighten. The next morning make out the rusk, lighten them again, and bake them when sufficiently light. This is a most excellent receipt.

Plain Sugar Cake.

Three pints of flour, rub into it one teacup of butter, three cups of sugar, one cup of milk, four eggs, two teaspoonsful of yeast-powder mixed in with the flour. Flavor to taste.

Queen's Cake.

One pound of flour, one pound of white sugar, half a pound of butter, six eggs, one teacupful of cream, one nutmeg, one wineglass of brandy, cream the butter and sugar together, then add the cream, then the eggs, then the flour, and lastly stir in the brandy.

Raised Doughnuts.

One quart of sugar, a scant pint of lard, one pint of milk, one pint of water; make into a sponge with a cup of yeast, four eggs. Make into a sponge at noon, let it rise until bedtime, then add flour enough to knead out soft, a little salt, one-half a teaspoonful of soda, one nutmeg. Let it stand until morning, then roll and cut out small in order to let them rise again, until they will float in hot lard (even if you have to wait to 10 A. M. to fry them). The knack is to get them light enough. Roll in pulverized sugar.

Soft Ginger Bread.

One cup of sugar, one cup of butter, one and a half cups of molasses, four eggs, one teaspoonful of soda, one of ginger, and two of cinnamon, and stir in flour sufficient to mix it.

Sponge Cake.

One pound and a half of eggs, one pound and a half of sugar, three-quarters of a pound of flour, the grated rind and juice of two lemons.

Sugar Cakes.

Four eggs, one pound sugar, one teacup butter, one teacup milk, one teaspoon soda, one of cream of tartar, flour enough to roll.

Sugar Cakes (another).

Six eggs, four and a half cups light-brown sugar, one cup milk, one cup butter, half cup lard, one teaspoon soda, one of cream of tartar, flour enough to roll.

Superior Chocolate Cake.

Cream together two cups of sugar, and one of butter, then add one cup of milk, half cake of Baker's chocolate (grated). Put in five well-beaten eggs. and three cups of flour into which you have stirred three teaspoonsful of yeast powder, adding the eggs and flour alternately.

Filling for the above.—One pound of pulverized sugar, with water enough to wet it. Beat the whites of three eggs a little, but not to a stiff froth; add the sugar, then half a cake of chocolate grated. Boil until it thickens, and after removing from the fire, and it cools a little, stir in a grated cocoanut. Flavor with vanilla.

Swiss Cake.

Take butter, flour, and sugar, of each the weight of four eggs. Beat together the yolks and sugar, add ten drops of essence of lemon, and a large teaspoonful of rose-water, add the butter just melted, and slowly sift in the flour, beating it until well mixed. Then stir in the whites (beaten stiff), and beat hard for a few minutes. Butter the tin and bake cake half an hour.

Tea Cakes.

Rub four ounces of butter into eight ounces of flour, eight ounces of currants, six ounces fine sugar, two yolks and one white of egg, and a spoonful of brandy; roll the paste and cut with a wineglass.

Washington Cake.

One cup of sugar, three eggs, one cup of yeast, one teacup melted butter, one pint new milk; make it a thick batter.

White Cake.

One pound of flour, the same of sugar, three-quarters of a pound of butter, the whites of fourteen eggs; flavor with peach-water or blanched almonds; use three teaspoonsful of yeast powder. If baked in a large cake, bake one hour.

White Mountain Cake.

One cup butter and three cups sugar creamed well together, half cup sweet milk, one teaspoon of cream of tartar in three and a half cups of flour, half teaspoon of soda in a little water, whites of ten eggs beaten very light; flavor with almond. Put flour in last. Bake in three jelly tins. When cool, put icing over each cake, and grated cocoanut over the icing. Place the cakes together, then ice, and grate cocoanut over the top and sides.

Variety Cake.

The whites of five eggs, two cups pulverized sugar, two cups and a half of flour, three-quarters of a cup of butter, one cup of sweet milk, three teaspoonsful of baking powder. Flavor with vanilla. Take four tablespoonsful of this dough, and to it add half cup molasses, half cup raisins, a few currants, and half cup flour. Bake like jelly cake, dividing the white dough into two cakes, putting the fruit cake between with layers of tart jelly.

DESSERTS.

A Plain Pudding (without eggs).

Three cups flour, one cup molasses, two of suet, one of milk, half pound raisins (cut), half pound currants, two teaspoons cream of tartar rubbed through the flour, half teaspoon soda dissolved in the milk. Steam four hours in a covered buttered pudding mould. Wine sauce.

Apple Charlotte.

Butter several thin slices of bread and line the sides of a deep earthen dish with them, always placing the buttered side next the dish. Then put in a layer (about two inches thick) of apples sliced up thin, put on the top of this sugar sprinkled thickly, and three cloves. Then another layer of bread and butter, then apples, and so on with alternate layers until the dish is full. Finally butter bread, lay it on a plate, pour some milk over it, lift carefully, and place it on the top of the whole, cover with a plate, put a weight on it, and let it bake slowly two hours. No sauce.

Apple Fritters.

Four pints of finely chopped apples, four eggs, a teaspoonful of salt, one pint and a half of

water, sixteen heaping tablespoonsful of flour.
Should the apples be very juicy, it may be found
necessary to add more flour. This same batter
makes an excellent pudding baked and eaten
with cream sauce or molasses.

Apple Méringue.

Stew your apples well and smoothly, sweeten
to taste, and add the rind of a lemon. Take the
whites of five eggs, beat to a stiff froth, put to
them a teacup of powdered sugar, a little rose-
water, and juice of the lemon. Put the fruit in
a flat dish and with a spoon put in the eggs.
Put into the oven to brown. A spoonful of
butter stirred in the apples while hot is an
improvement.

Apple Pudding.

A pint of apples stewed and mashed through
a colander; add a quarter of a pound of butter
and a quarter of a pound of sugar, five eggs
beaten light, orange-peel and rose-water to your
taste. Stick some citron on the top of your
pudding; bake in a paste.

Apple Sago.

Raw apples chopped fine, one quart of boiling
water, six tablespoonsful or quarter of a pound
of sago. Sweeten to taste, and add the rind
and juice of one lemon.

Baked Batter Pudding.

Five eggs well beaten, five even tablespoons of flour, five of milk to mix the flour. Add one quart of boiling milk. Bake fifteen minutes. Wine sauce.

Bird-Nest Pudding.

Take ten eggs, nine tablespoonsful of flour, one quart of milk. Take the core out of your apples, fill them with sugar, butter, and nutmeg. Place them in a pan and pour the batter over them. Bake until the apples are done.

Blackberry Pudding.

One-quarter of a pound of butter, the same of sugar and flour, a quarter of a pound also of grated bread, three pints of blackberries, three eggs, and a half teaspoonful of saleratus dissolved in a teaspoonful of cream, or one teaspoonful of yeast powder.

Blanc-Mange.

Three tablespoonsful of corn-starch mixed with a little milk, the yolks of four eggs beaten light, four tablespoonsful of sugar—when the milk boils pour it over the eggs, put in the corn-starch, and flavor with vanilla. This requires a quart of milk.

Bread Pudding.

Take two thick slices of bread across the loaf, pour boiling water over it, when soft pour off the water, mash the bread very fine, a piece of butter the size of an egg, two eggs, one cup sugar, one pint milk. Beat the sugar and eggs together, then stir in the milk; flavor to taste. Mix all together and bake it. In winter a piece of suet the size of an egg may be substituted for the butter, but *not* in summer.

Centennial Baked Apple Dumplings.

Take one pint of flour, a heaped tablespoonful of lard, two heaped teaspoonsful of yeast powder, a little salt, and sufficient milk to make a soft dough. Divide it into twelve portions, rolling each into a thin round cake. Chop fine sixteen apples, into which stir sufficient sugar to sweeten pleasantly, and half a grated nutmeg. Put into each cake of dough as much chopped apple as will fill it, and leave a margin for joining and forming into a ball. Put these balls into a deep pan or dish, and nearly cover them with water. Between each dumpling put a small piece of butter and a tablespoonful of sugar to make the sauce. Lastly, a small piece of butter on the top of each to brown them. Bake half hour.

4

Chocolate Blanc-Manje.

One quart of milk, three eggs, four ounces of chocolate, six tablespoonsful of white sugar, half box gelatine. Let the gelatine soak half hour in the milk; grate the chocolate and mix with a little milk. When the milk and gelatine begin to boil, stir in the chocolate – have the eggs and sugar well beaten together, then pour the boiling mixture on them, stirring all the time—return to the fire and let boil hard for ten minutes. Put in moulds to cool.

Cocoanut Pudding.

Two cocoanuts grated, half pound sugar, half pound butter, whites of eleven eggs, cream butter, sugar and eggs together, then add the cocoanuts. Bake in a paste.

Cocoanut Pudding.

Half pound of butter and half pound of fine sugar beaten to a cream, half pound of cocoanut grated fine, then add in the whites of six eggs beaten light. Rose-water to your taste. This quantity will make two puddings, baked in a paste.

Cottage Pudding.

One cup sugar, half cup butter beaten to a cream, one egg, two teaspoons cream of tartar well mixed in two cups flour, one teaspoon soda dissolved in one cup milk, and stirred in at the last when ready to put in the oven; season to taste. Bake half hour. Wine sauce.

Cottage Pudding.

Three cups of flour, one cup of sugar, one cup of milk, two tablespoonsful of butter, one tea-spoonful of yeast powder. Beat well together. Bake half an hour, and eat with sauce.

Crab Apple Jelly.

Pick and wash your apples, put them on with water enough to cover them well. Simmer until the skins peel off easily. Then take them from the fire, and allow three and three-quarters of a pound of white sugar to four pints of juice. Put the juice over the fire, and let it boil well, taking off the scum as it rises. After the scum ceases to rise, put in the sugar, and stir until it has all dissolved. Take from the fire and put it in small jelly glasses.

Cream Pie.

One cup sugar, one tablespoonful of butter, one cup and a half of flour, two-thirds of a cup of milk, one egg, two spoonsful of yeast powder. Roll. Beat together one egg, one tablespoonful corn-starch, one tablespoonful flour, and two of sugar. Stir it into a half pint of milk, and boil to thick custard. Flavor with vanilla. Spread and pile for cream pie.

Cream Puffs.

Six ounces of flour, four ounces of butter, four eggs, and one tumbler of cold water. Put the water into a pan with the butter, and let it come to a boil. Throw in the flour all at once, and let it boil until the flour is well cooked. When cold, add the eggs one at a time. Beat each one well into the flour, before adding the other. Drop tablespoonsful in muffin rings, and bake.

Cream for filling the above.—One tumbler of milk, half cup sugar, quarter of a cup of flour, one egg. Stir over the fire until it thickens. Flavor to taste. When the puffs are cold, split them, and fill with the cream.

Flavoring for Custards, Cakes, etc.

Take twenty drops of oil of bitter almonds, drop them on a small lump of magnesia. Place a funnel in the mouth of a bottle. Get a piece of "filtering paper" from a druggist. Rub smoothly together on the middle of this paper, the magnesia and oil of almonds. Place in the funnel, and over this pour one pint of cold water. When filtered it is ready for use. Any other essential oil may be prepared in the same manner.

Florindine.

Boil one quart of milk, stir in four table-spoons of rice-flour, let it boil ten minutes. Add one teacup of sugar, grated nutmeg or vanilla, a gill of cream, five eggs beaten separately until very light. Bake in paste.

Fritters.

Put a piece of butter the size of an egg into one pint of *boiling* water. Stir into this sufficient flour to make it very stiff. Beat smooth; as it cools, beat in five eggs (one at a time). Drop by spoonsful into hot lard. Serve with wine and sugar.

Foam Sauce.

One teacup sugar, two-thirds of a cup of butter, one teaspoonful of flour, beat smoothly; then place over fire and stir in three gills of boiling water, and flavor with wine or extract.

French Puff-Paste.

One pound of flour, a quarter of a pound of lard, a half pound of butter, and a half pint of water. This quantity will make two pies and two puddings.

Frozen Custard.

Take two quarts of milk, twelve eggs, and sixteen tablespoonsful of sugar, and make a custard; flavor when cold with vanilla, and then freeze as ice-cream.

Gelatine Jelly.

To a package of gelatine add one pint of cold water, the juice of three lemons and the rind of one. Let it stand one hour; then add two and a half pints of boiling water, one pint of wine, and two pounds of white sugar; strain and run into moulds. A tablespoonful of brandy improves it, and the flavor may be varied by the addition of three or four whole cloves or a stick or two of cinnamon.

Ground Corn Pudding.

Stir three-quarters of a pound of butter into two pounds of warm mush, then add the yolks of six eggs, the juice of two lemons, and the rind of one, with sugar, and spice to taste. Bake in paste.

Grits Pudding.

Take one cup grits, boil it; when boiled add a piece of butter the size of an egg, one quart milk, four eggs, half nutmeg, one wineglass of wine. Bake in an earthen dish. Ornament with spots of currant jelly. This quantity makes two good-sized puddings.

Hen's Nest.

Get fine eggs, make a hole at one end and empty the shells, fill with blanc-mange. When stiff and cold take off the shells. Pare the yellow rinds from six lemons, boil them in water till tender, then cut in strips to resemble straw, and preserve in sugar. Fill a small dish half full of nice jelly, when it is set put the strips of lemon on it in the form of a nest, and lay the eggs on it. To make the blanc-mange: Break one ounce of isinglass into very small pieces, wash it well, and pour on one pint of boiling water. Next morning add one quart of milk, boil until the isinglass dissolves; strain it, put in two ounces of sweet almonds pounded; sweeten it, and put it in the egg-shells. Julep straws can be used instead of the lemon strips.

Iced Apples.

Pare and core twelve large apples, fill with sugar, very little butter and cinnamon, bake till nearly done. Let them cool, and, if you can without breaking, put on another dish, if not, pour off the juice, have some icing prepared, lay on top and sides, and set into the oven a minute or two to brown slightly. Serve with cream.

Irene Spanish Cream.

Take half box gelatine to a quart of milk, let it dissolve in the milk while heating, which is best stirred all the time to prevent burning. Beat the yolks of four eggs with five tablespoonsful of sugar. As soon as the milk boils, pour it on the beaten yolks, and return to the fire, stirring all the time. As soon as it comes to the consistency of custard, have ready the well-beaten whites, and when the custard has been two or three minutes off the fire, stir the whites in thoroughly. Flavor to taste. Pour into moulds, which have been dipped in cold water.

Jelly (without boiling).

To one package of " Cox's Sparkling Gelatine," add one pint of cold water, the juice of three lemons, and the rinds pared very thin. Let it stand one hour, then add three pints of boiling water, half pint wine, and one and a half pounds white sugar. When the sugar is dissolved, strain the lemon rinds out, and set it away to cool.

Lemon Méringue.

Two large lemons (rind and juice), two teacups sugar, one teacup milk, two tablespoons corn-starch dissolved in the milk, yolks of six eggs. Beat the yolks light, add the sugar and lemon, and milk with corn-starch. Place in a paste, and bake it. Beat the whites of the eggs to a stiff froth with eight tablespoons of sugar, put it on the pie, and replace in the oven until it is a light brown.

Lemon Pudding.

Three potatoes boiled and well mashed, rind of three and juice of two lemons, half a pound butter, half a pound sugar, yolks of eleven eggs. Cream the sugar, butter, and eggs together, then add lemon and potato.

Lemon Pudding.

The juice and rind of one lemon, one cup of sugar, the yolks of two eggs, three tablespoonsful of flour, and milk to fill the plate. Méringue.

Méringue Pudding.

Pour one quart of boiling milk upon one pint of grated bread crumbs, one teacup of granulated sugar, one teaspoonful of salt, a lump of butter the size of an egg, and the grated rind of one lemon. Stir well, and when cool add the well-beaten yolks of six eggs. Pour this mixture in a buttered dish and bake. When it is done, let it stand until cold, then pour over it a méringue formed of the whites of six eggs, two cups of pulverized sugar, and juice of one lemon. Put it in a hot oven until browned over the top.

Mince Meat Pudding.

One pint and a half of milk, six eggs, and as much bread as will make it sufficiently thick, three or four tablespoonsful of mince meat, one quarter of a pound of butter, and spice and sugar to your taste. Baked without paste.

Orange Jelly.

One half package of gelatine, half pint cold water, half pint boiling water, two cups of

sugar, juice of five oranges, and two lemons.
Strain into moulds.

Peach Ice Cream.

Pare a half peck of peaches, and wash them;
sweeten them with a pound and a half of sugar,
and stir in two quarts of milk; then freeze.

Plombiere.

One pint of scalded milk, one pint of cream,
one teaspoonful isinglass, one handful seedless
raisins, one ounce of citron, shreds of preserved
pineapple, ginger, or cherries, four tablespoonsful of wine; sugar to your taste, a little extract
of almonds, the whites of four eggs beaten stiff.
Freeze as ice cream.

Plum Pudding.

Thirteen eggs, one pound of sugar, a small
loaf of stale bread (grated), one pound of raisins, one pound of currants, one pound of suet,
a quarter of a pound of citron, and a handful
of flour.

Plum Pudding (without eggs).

One cup molasses, one cup suet, one cup milk,
one teaspoon soda, one pound raisins, as much
flour as will make a very stiff batter. Boil two
hours, and serve with any kind of sauce.

Potato Pudding.

One pound finely mashed potatoes, quarter pound butter, quarter pound sugar, half nutmeg, three eggs. Bake in paste without a top crust, or in a deep dish without any paste.

Pudding Sauce.

One cup of sugar, half a cup of butter, half a pint of boiling water, a little thickening of flour; boil a few minutes and add one egg well beaten, flavor with brandy, or wine, or nutmeg. This cannot be excelled.

Puff Paste.

One pound and a quarter of sifted flour, one pound of butter cut in quarters; take a pound of flour, and with a knife cut fine one of the quarters of butter into the flour, wet it with half a pint of ice-water, then roll it out and lay in the other quarter of butter in small pieces, and dredge a part of the remaining flour over the butter, and roll again, so continuing until the butter is all used.

Rice Coquettes.

One teacup of rice, boiled in a pint of milk and the same of water, until quite tender and very dry; while hot add a piece of butter the size of an egg, two tablespoonsful of white sugar, two eggs, juice and grated peel of one lemon, or essence of lemon; stir well and dry on the stove. Have ready the yolks of two eggs beaten on a plate, some fine cracker crumbs on another, make up the rice into rolls, dip first in the egg, then the cracker, and fry in hot lard to a light brown; sprinkle powdered sugar over them.

Rice-Flour Pudding.

Put to boil one quart of milk, reserving a tea-cupful to mix five tablespoonsful of rice flour. When the milk boils, put in the mixed flour, and stir it until it thickens a little. When slightly cool, stir in a quarter of a pound of butter, and the well-beaten yolks of four eggs, with six tablespoonsful of white sugar. When ready to bake, mix in the whites of the eggs whipped to a stiff froth. Flavor with the juice and grated rind of a lemon, or a glass of rose-water.

Rice Pudding (without eggs).

Wash a small coffee cup of rice and put it into three pints of milk over night, in the morning add a piece of butter half the size of

5

an egg, one teacup of sugar, a little salt, nutmeg and cinnamon; bake two and a half hours. After it has become hot enough to melt the butter, stir it from the bottom (without moving the dish); if raisins are to be used stir them in now.

Riz-au-Lait.

Soak two tablespoons of rice in a quart of milk. When soaked, add one saltspoon of salt, a small stick of cinnamon, half cup sugar. Place in a well-heated oven. Cook slowly two hours.

Sally Lunn; or, Cake Pudding.

Take a piece of butter the size of an egg, and cream with two cups of sugar—then of a cup of sweet milk add half—mix well and stir in one cup of flour, then the other half of milk and a second cup of flour. Of four eggs well beaten add one-half, and then the third cup of flour—then the remaining half of eggs and the fourth cup of flour, in which must be put a teaspoonful of yeast powder. The whole well beaten and put in the oven to bake—will take an hour or so. This makes a nice Sally Lunn for supper, or, eaten with cold sauce, makes a nice dessert.

Snow Pudding.

Half box gelatine, half pint of cold water—
let it soak half hour—then add half pint boiling
water. When cold, add the whites of three
eggs beaten a little, two cups of sugar, juice
of two lemons. Beat three-quarters of an hour.
Put in moulds to cool; make a custard of the
yolks and flavor with vanilla, to eat over it.

Superior Mince-Meat.

One pound of chopped meat, one pound and
a half of chopped suet, two pounds of raisins,
two pounds of currants, half pound of citron,
half teaspoonful ground cloves, two orange
rinds dried and pounded, one tablespoonful
ground ginger, one of cinnamon and allspice
(mixed), one teaspoonful of mace, one dozen
pippin apples chopped fine, three pounds of
sugar, one pint of wine, one pint of cider, one
pint of brandy, and a little salt.

Tapioca and Apples.

Soak two tablespoons of tapioca in one pint
of water three hours, then sweeten it with one
cup of sugar. Pare and core twelve pippin
apples, fill with sugar, pour the tapioca over
them, and bake. When done, grate nutmeg
over the top.

Vanilla Sauce.

To three pints of milk stir in one tablespoonful of flour or arrowroot, the yolks of six eggs well beaten. Stir until it boils. Sweeten to taste, and flavor strongly with vanilla. Use when cold.

Whortleberry Pudding.

Two cups of sugar, five eggs, three cups of flour, half cup cream; make up thick with whortleberries. Add a little yeast powder. Bake or boil several hours.

PICKLES.

Black Walnut Pickles.

Take them in the spring when you can run a needle easily through them. First wash and wipe them, then stick them all over with a large needle. Take three large onions and stick them full of cloves. Put your walnuts in a stone jar, arranging them with one of the onions at the bottom, one in the middle, and one at the top, then cover the whole with cold vinegar, and tie the jar over closely to exclude the air. The longer you can keep them before using, the better you will find them, as age improves them.

Chow-Chow Pickle.

Eight heads cabbage, six large onions, cut and salt over night. Press the water from this, then add two pounds sugar, one ounce mace, two ounces cinnamon, one-quarter ounce cloves, two ounces celery seed, one ounce ginger, two ounces turmeric, six green and six red peppers (having removed the seed); add enough cold vinegar to cover the whole.

Chow-Chow.

Two colanders cut tomatoes, six large peppers, one colander sliced onions, one colander or thirty-six cucumbers (sliced), two ounces of mace, two tablespoonsful ground black pepper, half pound of mustard seed, two tablespoonsful ginger, two tablespoonsful of mustard, one ounce of celery seed, one pint of salt, one pound of sugar, half gallon of vinegar, two ounces of black mustard seed, two tablespoonsful of allspice. Boil hard one hour; stir well to prevent burning; when done add two tablespoonsful of turmeric.

Cucumber Catsup, No. 1.

Pare your cucumbers closely and grate them. Season to your taste with salt, pepper, and vinegar. Mix and put in bottles, which without corking you will place in a vessel of cold water and set on the stove, letting the water boil for two or three hours, until the catsup is done.

Cucumber Catsup, No. 2.

Three dozen full-grown cucumbers, one dozen onions; cut the cucumbers and onions in small pieces, sprinkle them with salt, and let them stand twenty-four hours. Then drain off the water, put to them mace, cloves, and cayenne pepper. Cover them with cold vinegar, and pour over a little sweet oil to exclude the air.

Cucumber Pickles.

Wash and wipe two hundred cucumbers, place them in stone jars. Make a pickle that will bear an egg, boil it, and pour boiling hot over the cucumbers, and some peppers. Cover the jars with a double cloth, plate, and weight, and let them remain twenty-four hours. Then take them out, and wipe them dry. After drying the jars return the pickles to them. Boil the vinegar with whatever spices you like, mustard seed, cloves of garlic, one pound brown sugar, and pour boiling hot over the pickles. The sugar strengthens the vinegar, without leaving a sweet taste on the pickles.

Cucumber Pickles (quickly made).

Wash and drain the cucumbers, then place them in your jar, with a large onion stuck with cloves. Cover them with strong scalding brine, and let them stand twenty-four hours; then pour it off, and take sufficient vinegar to fill the jar, put it in your preserving kettle with a small lump of alum, a teacup of white mustard seed, one tablespoonful of cloves, one of allspice, two of black pepper, put it over the fire, and let it boil a few minutes, then pour it over the cucumbers while scalding hot. Tie them up immediately.

Cucumber Sauce.

Three dozen cucumbers, eight large onions chopped fine, and add one cup and a half of salt. Place in a colander to drain eight hours, then add half cup of black pepper, half pound of white mustard seed, and three pints of vinegar. Mix well together, bottle for use. The size of the cucumbers regulates somewhat the quantity of vinegar; medium size preferred.

East India Pickle.

Cut fine one white cabbage, four or five onions, a root of horseradish. With this take radish pods, beans, cauliflowers, small onions, large and small cucumbers, green peppers, and anything else you like. Soak all in salt and water twenty-four hours. When drained, boil your vinegar with red peppers, white and brown mustard seed, one quarter pound of each. When boiling hot, pour it over the pickle. Mix one pint bowl of mustard as for the table, and mix it into the pickle, also one teaspoon of cayenne pepper and one of mace.

French Pickle.

One peck green tomatoes, one quarter peck onions, slice them and sprinkle thickly with salt, and let them stand twenty-four hours. One quarter pound mustard seed, one ounce cloves, one ounce allspice, one quarter pound mixed mustard, two tablespoons of ground black pepper, one of red pepper, one ounce celery seed, one pound brown sugar, three quarts vinegar. Cook slowly for three or four hours. Mix the mustard with vinegar, and pour over the pickle when cold.

Mangoes (Sweet Pickle).

Fill a three-gallon jar with mangoes and cucumbers and cover them with strong brine.

After letting them stand several days pour off the brine, and boil it and pour it hot over the pickles again. Do this every third morning until you have scalded them three times. You are then to mix equal quantities of vinegar and water and scald them three times as before. Keep them covered with cabbage leaves to keep in the steam. To prepare the stuffing for the mangoes, take one teacup of black pepper, one of allspice, one and a half of ginger, one ounce of cloves, and one of mace; beat them, but not fine. Take half of the spices after they are beaten, reserving the other half for the cucumbers. Add one small cabbage chopped, one pint black mustard seed, one of white, two cups scraped horseradish, two pounds and a half of brown sugar. Mix all well, and fill the mangoes, adding to the stuffing half teacup celery seed. Take the other half of the spices, with two pounds and a half more sugar, and boil them with as much vinegar as will cover the three gallons of pickles. Pour it on hot.

Spanish Pickle.

Three dozen large cucumbers, four large green peppers, half peck onions, half peck green tomatoes cut in pieces. Sprinkle with one pint of salt, and let it stand all night. Drain the next morn-

ing, and add one ounce of mace, one ounce of
white pepper, one ounce white mustard seed,
half ounce of cloves, one pound and a half of
brown sugar, and one piece of horseradish.
Cover with vinegar and boil half hour.

Sweet Pickled Damsons.

Take seven pounds damsons, wipe dry, add
one ounce cinnamon, one ounce cloves, put a
layer of each in a jar. Then boil one quart of
sharp vinegar with three pounds of sugar, skim
it, and pour it boiling hot over the damsons,
let them stand twenty-four hours. The next
day pour the juice off, boil it again and pour it
over the damsons. After they stand another
twenty-four hours, boil the whole, just scalding
the fruit. Place in jars when quite cold, and
cover them with the syrup.

Sweet Pickled Peaches.

Take eighteen pounds of peaches, rub them
with a coarse towel (or pare them), halve them.
Put eight pounds sugar into one quart of vinegar, a handful of cloves, a handful of stick cinnamon, one tablespoon mace.

Place the sugar, vinegar, and spice into the
preserving kettle. When it boils, throw in

the peaches, boil until clear, remove the peaches, and boil the syrup until it thickens.

Sweet Pickled Strawberries.

One pound and a half of sugar, half pint of vinegar, two quarts of picked berries. Boil the sugar and vinegar, skim it well, and while boiling pour in the berries, let them simmer twenty-five or thirty minutes, then remove the berries, being careful not to mash them, and let the syrup boil a half hour longer. Put in the fruit, just allow it to heat, and pour all into your glasses.

Tomato Catsup.

Choose those that are round, halve them, take out the green core, put on the fire in a bell-metal kettle; when bursted, pass through a sieve; let stand until the water settles on the top, pour off one-third of the water; and to every gallon of tomatoes add not quite one-fourth pound of *whole* allspice, a stick of horseradish, a scant tablespoon cayenne pepper, a little *whole* mace, and six onions, salt to taste, one-half pint strong vinegar. Boil until it thickens in the spoon, pass through a colander; to each bottle add one clove of garlic; bottle it when cool, cork tight, and dip the corked bottle into a cement composed of equal parts of rosin and beeswax. Shake before using. Keep in a dark place.

Tomato Soy.

One and a half pecks of green tomatoes, half a peck of onions, one large pint of salt; slice the tomatoes and onions, sprinkle the salt over, and let them stand twenty-four hours; drain off all the water, and boil twenty minutes in weak vinegar and water, then drain; boil three pints of vinegar and four pounds and a half of brown sugar; spices, one tablespoonful of ginger, two tablespoonsful of cinnamon, one tablespoonful of cloves, two of mace, two of black pepper, and four of celery seed, also three of mustard; mix the mustard as for table use, and stir it into the vinegar; put in the tomatoes and onions, and let them get hot through.

PRESERVES.

Apple Jelly.

To one peck of sour, juicy apples, take two quarts of water, boil the apples until they are perfectly soft, then strain through flannel. To one pint of juice add one pint of sugar; after the sugar is dissolved strain again, and boil rapidly until done. Have ready two large fresh lemons cut in slices, over which pour the jelly boiling hot. Fine, sour, juicy apples, although they may be red, will make equally as nice jelly as lighter ones.

Blackberry Syrup.

Extract the juice from the blackberries, and to every quart of strained juice allow three-quarters of a pound of loaf sugar, a heaped teaspoonful of powdered cinnamon, the same of cloves, and a large nutmeg, grated; mix the spices with the juice and sugar, and boil in a porcelain kettle, skimming it well; when cold, stir into each quart of made syrup half a pint of fourth-proof brandy, then bottle for use.

Preserved Burr Cucumbers.

Take out the insides and let them lie in salt and water four days, then soak them in fresh water two hours, then boil them in fresh water with a small lump of alum and a few peach leaves, then boil in clear water, then make a syrup, allowing five pounds of sugar to four pounds of cucumbers, flavoring with lemon and ginger to your taste, in which *boil* your cucumbers until perfectly done.

6

Preserved Pineapple.

Pare and slice the pineapple, and to every pound of fruit put three-quarters of a pound of sugar, and a pint of water to every pound of sugar; make a syrup, and boil and skim until clear, then add your fruit and boil until clear, tender, and done.

Pineapple Marmalade.

Pare the pineapple and cut out the eyes, and grate; then to every pound of fruit add three-quarters of a pound of sugar, and boil until clear and done.

Preserved Cantaloupe.

Cut the cantaloupe in slices and take off the rind; to eight pounds of fruit allow six pounds of sugar, one pound of green ginger, and four lemons.

Preserved Limes.

Take the limes when green, put them in strong salt and water (strong enough to bear an egg), for six weeks or longer. Then put them in fresh cold water for twenty-four hours, changing the water every three hours. Cut them in halves, and clean them entirely of pulp, simmer them in saleratus water, until perfectly tender (one teaspoonful to six quarts of water), put them again in cold water for twenty-four hours, changing often. To each pound of fruit two pounds and a half of sugar, and two pints of water. Boil the syrup fifteen or twenty minutes before you put in the limes. Boil the whole one hour and twenty minutes.

To Can Pineapple.

Pare the fruit, then tear the meat from the stalk with a fork. To six pounds of fruit put two pounds of sugar. Cook thirty minutes. Then can.

To Can Quinces.

Take the parings and cores from one peck of quinces, and boil them well. Strain the liquor through a bag, and to this put five pounds sugar, then add the quinces, and boil till tender. Then can.

To Preserve the Heart of Watermelon.

To one pound of fruit take one-half pound of white sugar, and to the fruit of one watermelon, put the rinds of six lemons, pared and cut into shreds, a few blades of mace.

Boil the fruit until clear, and boil the syrup until it thickens. Ginger is sometimes preferred for flavoring instead of lemon.

To Preserve Pears.

Pare and (if large) halve them, leaving the stems on. Place in a syrup of one pound of sugar and one-half pint of water, one pound of pears, with some green ginger and sliced lemon. Boil until clear, but boil the syrup one half hour after the pears are done.

To Preserve Citron.

Cut the citron into pieces the size and shape you fancy. Pare the green rind off. Place the citron in water, with two tablespoons of salt, and let it stand all night.

The next morning put it in clear cold water and soak one hour. Place the citron in another water in the preserving kettle, with a lump of alum half the size of an egg, and boil it until somewhat tender. Remove the fruit, and put it once more into clear cold water for one hour. To six pounds of fruit put seven and a half pounds of sugar, juice of two lemons, and the rind pared very thin and cut into shreds, six cloves, two small sticks of cinnamon, and ginger to your taste. Boil until clear and tender.